Electric
from TIDES

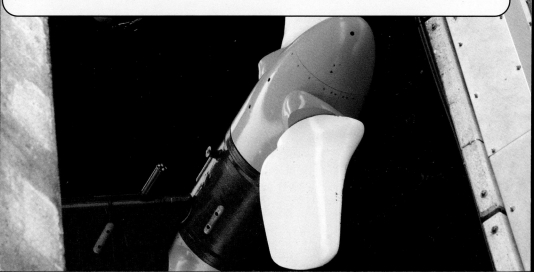

Making electricity

We can make electricity.

The tide

Look at the water.

The water goes in.

The water goes out.

The water goes in and out.
In and out, in and out,
day after day.

The paddles

Look at the **paddles**.

The paddles go in the water.

The paddles go

round and round in the water.

The tide and the paddles

The water goes in and out,

day after day.

The paddles go round

and round and round.

11

The paddles will go round and round all day. This will make electricity.

The electricity is made here.

Glossary

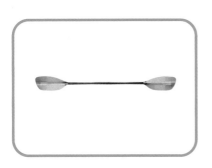 paddles

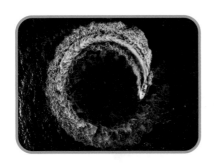 round and round